Marie and Bruce

Marie and Bruce

A PLAY BY WALLACE SHAWN

Grove Press, Inc., New York

Copyright © 1980 by Wallace Shawn

All Rights Reserved

No part of this book may be reproduced, stored in a retrieval system, or transmitted, in any form, by any means, electronic, mechanical, photocopying, recording, or otherwise, without the prior written permission of the publisher.

CAUTION: This play is fully protected, in whole, in part, or in any form, under the Copyright Laws of the United States of America, the British Empire, including the Dominion of Canada, and all other countries of the Copyright Union, and is subject to royalty. All rights, including professional, amateur, motion picture, recitation, radio, television, and public reading are strictly reserved. All inquiries concerning such rights should be addressed to the author's agent: Audrey Wood, International Creative Management, 40 West 57th Street, New York, N.Y. 10019.

First Evergreen Edition 1980
First Printing 1980
ISBN: 0-394-17661-8
Grove Press ISBN: 0-8021-4308-3
Library of Congress Catalog Card Number: 80-991

LIBRARY OF CONGRESS CATALOGING IN
PUBLICATION DATA

Shawn, Wallace.
Marie and Bruce.

I. Title.
PS3569.H387M3   1980   812'.54   80-991
ISBN 0-394-17661-8 (pbk.)

Manufactured in the United States of America

Distributed by Random House, Inc., New York

GROVE PRESS, INC., 196 West Houston Street
New York, N.Y. 10014

To Deborah

LONDON PRODUCTION
First performance in the Theatre Upstairs at the Royal Court, July 13, 1979.

MARIE	Stephanie Fayerman
BRUCE	Philip Donaghy
HERB/FRED/WAITER	Paul Kember
ENID/JEAN	Robin Pappas
BETTINA/ILSA/ROXANNE	Annie Hayes
HENRY/ED/TIM	Paul Jesson
ANTOINE/BERT	Robert Hamilton

DIRECTED by Les Waters
DESIGNED by Peter Hartwell
LIGHTING by Rory Dempster
SOUND by Peter Deacon
STAGE MANAGER Vandra Edwards
DEPUTY STAGE MANAGER Jamie Rix
ARTISTIC DIRECTOR, ROYAL COURT THEATRE Stuart Burge

NEW YORK PRODUCTION

First performance in the Newman Theater, New York Shakespeare Festival Public Theater, January 8, 1980.

MARIE	Louise Lasser
BRUCE	Bob Balaban
HENRY/TIM/ED	Griffin Dunne
ANTOINE/WAITER	Tom Costello
HERB/MAX (at table with Bert and Ed)	Frank Modell
ENID/ILSA	Angela Pietropinto
BETTINA	Sakina Jaffrey
JEAN	Parker McCormick
FRED/BERT	John Ferraro

DIRECTED by Wilford Leach
SCENERY by Jim Clayburgh and Wilford Leach
COSTUMES by Patricia McGourty
LIGHTING by Martin Tudor
PRODUCTION STAGE MANAGER Peter Dowling
STAGE MANAGER Jaqueline Yancey
ASSISTANT TO MR. LEACH Jack Chandler
PRODUCER Joseph Papp

NOTE:

Apart from the actors playing MARIE and BRUCE, three additional men and two additional women are required to cover the smaller parts:

1st man: HERB, FRED, and the WAITER.
2nd man: HENRY, ED, and TIM.
3rd man: ANTOINE and BERT.
1st woman: ENID and JEAN.
2nd woman: BETTINA, ILSA, and ROXANNE.

The ages of the characters are as follows:

MARIE and BRUCE are in their early thirties.
HERB is in his thirties or forties.
FRED is in his thirties.
The WAITER is in his thirties.
HENRY is in his thirties or forties.
ED is in his thirties or forties.
TIM is about thirty.
ANTOINE is in his forties.
BERT is in his late forties.
ENID is in her late twenties.
JEAN is in her twenties.
BETTINA is in her late twenties.
ILSA is in her early thirties.
ROXANNE is in her twenties.

The entrances and exits of BRUCE and the WAITER, and the entrance (but not the exit) of BERT and ED, are indicated in the script. Otherwise the script doesn't mention entrances and exits. Characters appear for their brief moments and then disappear, but the script doesn't indicate exactly how or when they do so. Similarly, although the play does "take place" in certain places, the script doesn't indicate exactly when or how these should be represented. Characters and things should be present when they ought to be, and not when they shouldn't be, but the appearance and disappearance of characters and things should be accomplished in a way that does not detract from the smooth and continuous flow of the play.

Complete and detailed sets are clearly not required. The characters should be dressed in contemporary clothes.

As the play opens, MARIE *is wearing a flowery dress.* BRUCE *is asleep, in his pajamas.* MARIE *has just gotten up. It is morning.*

MARIE *(to audience)*: Let me tell you something. I find my husband so God damned irritating that I'm planning to leave him. And that's a fact. *(To* BRUCE*)* Yes! I'm sick of you! Do you get it? You're driving me insane! I can't stand living with you for one more minute! I'm sick of it! I hate it! I hate my life with you! Do you hear me? I hate it!

BRUCE: Oh—hello, darling. Is it time to get up?

MARIE: No! No! God damn you, it's the middle of the night! Now go back to sleep—please!

BRUCE: Well, don't be irritable, darling—

MARIE: Irritable? Irritable? You call me *irritable?* God damn you, I've had about *enough* of your disgusting *insults,* you God damned cheap God damned idiotic pig, you shit! Now go back to sleep!

BRUCE: Well—all right, darling—

He returns to sleep.

MARIE *(to audience again)*: Let's begin at the beginning. Yesterday morning this fucking pig woke me up from a good night's sleep to ask me—to ask me where his God damned horrible piece-of-shit two-hundred-year-old typewriter was. I threw your typewriter *out,* you God damned fucking incredible pig! I threw it *out* because it makes too much noise! Get yourself *another* typewriter that doesn't make any *noise,* I told him, you God damned son of a *bitch,* you idiot, you *shit.* Do you get it? Get yourself *another* typewriter that doesn't make any *noise.* "But now, darling, after all, I *need* my little typewriter"—you pathetic pig, you piece of shit, you idiot! You need your little typewriter? Poor little man needs his tiny little whatsit?— God damn you, you pig! "Well, darling, really—" Well, *darling, darling—* You God damned worthless piece of filthy shit, you idiot, you asshole, you God damned filthy cock-sucking turd! *(To audience)* I'll tell you frankly I'm fed *up* with this God damned fucking incredible pig, I've *had* it with him, I've had it up to *here*, and I'm going to fuckin' well leave him and see how he likes it.

BRUCE *(waking, half-asleep)*: Darling, don't be angry. I'm a nice guy—I am—I'm not so bad. All right, I'm worthless, I'm nothing—I know that. But why can't you accept me? I'm only a person.

MARIE: Oh, really? Is that it? You mean you're only a person? Well then pardon my mistake. You're only a person? Well, *pardon* my mistake—I just thought you were a *shit*, you filthy cock-sucking turd— Now do you have to lie there in that disgusting *heap?* I mean if you're going to get up and start wrecking my whole fucking day, then please get *out* of that *bed* and *get* some of that filth out of the sink and make me some breakfast! Now! Now! Now! I said, now!

BRUCE: Oh—you want some breakfast, darling?

MARIE: I said I want some breakfast. Would you like me to repeat it? I *want* some *breakfast*, I *want* some *breakfast*. Now do you think that might be possible? Or maybe it just *isn't* quite possible today. Or do you think it just *might* be possible? Eh, "honey"? A little coffee and a roll? Or is that too much to ask? A little bit *too* much, "darling"? A little bit *too* much to ask? Well, that's great! That's great! I'll just clean up the whole fucking thing myself, you fucking *pig*, you lazy *shit!*

BRUCE: Well, I could heat up the coffee—er—darling—really—

MARIE: Oh you could, could you? You mean you could actually walk over to the stove and actually turn on the heat under the coffee? Do you really mean it? Oh no—oh no, oh no, oh no, that's not *possible*—you just meant that you *might* be able to do it—I mean you *might* be able to do it, but actually you just *can't,* isn't that it, you shit? Isn't that what you meant?

BRUCE: Oh no—I can easily do it, darling— See, I'll just get it on here—and then those rolls over there—

MARIE: And would you mind putting on your little bathrobe so I don't have to look at those filthy, filthy, disgusting pajamas? Or is that *really* now too much to ask? I mean, I think it might be nice. *I* think so, really. *I* really do think so. I mean, don't you, "darling"? Or do you disagree? Oh well, I'm *so sorry*, I see you just don't agree— Well that's fine, that's fine, I don't mind looking at your pajamas, but just close them up tightly! Tightly! You sickening turd, you filthy little shit— "Yes, a horrible episode happened today. A disgusting, nauseating animal was seen wandering around in a person's apartment. A revolting dick protruding from his open pajamas revealed the filthy beast to be a male shit of the most disgusting variety. The intruding filth was immediately chopped into bits, and his revolting member was thrown into the stove where it was roasted. A neighbor's baby, coming upon the member and tasting a bite of it, developed an incurable plague and vomited his guts out."

BRUCE: Well, darling, I think I'll just slip on my clothes, actually.

He exits.

MARIE: "I think I'll just slip on my clothes, actually"—how cute, what a cute little fellow— "I think I'll just slip on my clothes, actually" —"I think I'll just slip on my clothes, actually"—"I think I'll just slip on my clothes, actually"— It was a miserable summer. It was hot. We didn't have jobs. We were running out of money. We didn't have anything to read that was good, it was all worthless shit. I had the flu the whole time—I was sick, I was weak, I felt dizzy—

He returns, dressed.

You God damned fucking son of a bitch, you pig, you shit, you revolting turd—

BRUCE: Now, darling, is this really—

MARIE: Shut up! I said shut up! Shut up!

BRUCE: Well—all right, darling—I was only—

MARIE: You God damned filthy son of a bitch, you incredible shit, you nauseating *turd*—

BRUCE: Well, here are the rolls—

MARIE: Oh boy, that's great. That's great. Just great. Really great. You're really quite a guy. A real man. A *real* man. *Watch out*— oh boy, here he comes!

BRUCE: Well—ah—darling—now you take this one—oh my, they are rather tasty, now, aren't they, darling?

Silence. They eat.

MARIE: Great. Just great. So what happens now? Eh, *"honey"?*

BRUCE: There were—

MARIE: Eh, "honey"? So what happens now? Eh, "honey"? Eh, "honey"?

BRUCE: Well actually, darling, I'd been planning to go out rather early today— You see, Roger and I thought we might have a quick lunch somewhere together—

MARIE: Oh, Roger, eh? Well, how fascinating— wow! The world's most interesting person! Boy, I wish I could be around for *that* lunch, I'll tell you— I mean, lunch with Roger— wow! gosh! Do you think he might tell you some of those great ideas he has about the history of urine and feces in the nineteenth century? Roger! Oh boy, what a brain! I just *love* to listen to Roger when he *really* gets going, I mean when he *really* gets into his groove, do you know what I mean? I mean, it's just so enriching just to hear his ideas come crawling right out of his very own mouth just right while you're sitting there next to him at the very same table. It's *really* a pleasure, it's *really* great. And do you know what's best about Roger? It's the fact that he's *so* boring that he even gets bored *himself,* so you can watch those little bits of drool just come creeping from the corners of his mouth—and do you know that little crinkly red look that he gets around the corners of his *eyes?* Well *that's* when you know that he's going to stop talking, because he's just run out of boring things to say, so then *you* have to talk for a moment while he tries to think up a few *more* boring things to say— Oh God— Roger—oh, he's *really* great. Of course I'm a little bit jealous now, you know, because, after all, I mean, to think that you'll be sitting there hearing Roger's ideas about feces and shit, and I'll be missing them—I mean —to think that you just selfishly made your plans to go out with *my* favorite person just all by yourself, just leaving me at home to just sit here and think about all the little things that I might be missing— But well— I forgive you—I know you men need time to yourselves, just to suck each other off in your own little ways—

BRUCE: But, darling, I really think I'd better get ready to meet Roger. I mean, you won't mind, will you, my love, if I just shave a bit and brush my teeth now? Did you need to use the bathroom? Am I getting in your way?

MARIE: Why, no! Not at all! Getting in my way? *You* get in *my* way?—aha ha ha ha! What a funny idea! As if that could happen! Oh—God—you really are funny—

BRUCE: All right then, darling, I'll see you in a moment.

He exits.

MARIE *(to audience)*: All right, so what happened then, after I threw out the typewriter? It was two hundred years old, it was a wreck, it was filthy—he went downstairs into the trash, and he looked and he looked, but he could not find his filthy little machine. So he came upstairs in his torn little sweater, and he put his head on my chest, and he cried. And he cried and he cried and he cried and he cried, and I finally thought, Well, I really have to leave you. I mean, you're a fine little man, you're not a bad little man, but, I mean, I really have to leave you, and I really have to leave you, and there's really just nothing else to say. And that's when I decided that I had to leave him.

BRUCE *enters.*

BRUCE: Hi, darling.

MARIE: Hi, Bruce.

BRUCE: Do you think we should throw out this coffee? Or keep it one more day?

MARIE: Oh, I don't know, Bruce. What would *you* say about it? Let's hear *your* opinion. Keep it for a day?—or just toss it out?

BRUCE: Well, why don't I make a fresh pot right now—just so you'll have some?

MARIE: Why, Bruce, how thoughtful! *I* didn't know you were a saint—that's really just terrific—you make a *perfect* saint.

BRUCE: Oh well—thank you—er—darling—I'll just do this quickly.

He starts to make the coffee. Silence.

MARIE: Bruce—darling—I think you smell of urine, sweetheart. *(He keeps working on the coffee.)* I say, sweetheart, I believe your trousers have urine on them, dear. Do you think you should change them?

BRUCE: Darling, I'm trying to concentrate on making this coffee. Is that all right with you, sweetheart? Please don't disturb me.

MARIE: But, darling—your trousers have urine on them today, dearest. I think they should be changed—don't you?

BRUCE: I'm doing my best, darling. I'm doing my best. Simply the best that I can. Simply my best. Simply the best that I can. Now these *aren't* the trousers I'm planning to wear. I'm *planning* to change them. But I need my concentration. I need to pay attention to the thing that I'm doing. Do you follow me, darling?

MARIE: Yes, Bruce. I think I do, dear. I think I do, dearest.

BRUCE *exits*.

(To audience) We had arranged to go to Frank's for dinner, for a party. Frank was a

friend. I wanted to stay home. I had to talk to Bruce. *(To* BRUCE, *who immediately returns in new trousers)* You know, Bruce, sweetheart, do you really think we need to go to Frank's tonight, darling? Why don't we just stay home for the evening. I need to talk to you, sweetheart—it's been so long since we've talked. And I really have to talk to you about various things.

BRUCE: Well, darling, I know we haven't had much of a talk for a very long while, and that would be so nice, but you know, I really don't see how we can *avoid* going over to Frank's at this point—

MARIE: But, Bruce, do we really need to go there?

BRUCE: Well, darling, he's invited us, and as a matter of fact I really don't feel like going there at *all,* but I think we just *have* to. I mean, he did invite us, and we said we'd go there—and I mean, we said we *would* go, so I just don't really see how we can *avoid* going over there now, you see, at this point, really— But the thing is, darling, we can just stay briefly and then go along and have dinner somewhere pleasant and talk all we like. Now doesn't that sound nice?

MARIE: Yes, all right, Bruce. Whatever you want. Shall I meet you at Frank's, then?

BRUCE: Well yes, why don't you, darling? Why don't you just meet me there? And then we'll go out afterward to someplace nice and have a bite to eat, and just talk all we like. Now is that all right, darling? *(Silence.)* I love you, sweetheart. *(They kiss.)* Good-bye, darling. The coffee's almost ready.

MARIE: Good-bye, Bruce.

BRUCE: Good-bye, darling.

He exits. Silence.

MARIE: I was tired. I was sick. The apartment was filthy. The dishes were filthy. The bed was filthy. I had thrown out his typewriter. And now I planned to leave him. As soon as he left, I grabbed the sheets off the bed and hurled them onto the floor. The bed was stripped—but then I couldn't put on the new ones. I stood by the window. The heat was overpowering. What to do. I decided I would get very drunk at the party at Frank's. This was something to look forward to, at least. Then I'd finally tell Bruce I was planning to leave him. As for the rest of the day, I spent most of it getting ready to go out. I showered a couple of times; I put on my flowery dress; I put on lots of makeup. By the end of the day, I really looked great. I don't think anyone would have had a hard time if they'd had to look at me. Eventually I grew hungry, and a large sandwich, stuffed with vegetables *and* meat and some rather flavorful exotic hot sauce, took a great big bite out of my raging appetite. Strangely, it was not yet time to go to Frank's, so I decided to walk there by an indirect route. I went out onto the street and was shocked to find an attractive dog, bumping at my legs. When I reached down to pet him, his large tongue began lapping at my hand in a pleasing manner. He had a thin nose and gold and white fur and a face like a person. I was delighted. He followed me along until we reached a little gate that seemed to open onto an enormous garden. As my watch still told me I had plenty of time, and as the gate was clearly unlocked, I walked through it happily, followed by my trusty and slender and companionable dog. Inside, the flowers were huge. They grew to a great height, and their petals were gigantic and robust. There were purples, reds, and oranges, and countless shades of peach, all competing for our attention, and it was truly amazing how thick and hardy each blossom seemed to be. And then the perfume of the flowers as well was terrific and potent, and a desire to sit down in the midst of these flowers and see how they would tower over my head became irresistible. I threw my raincoat down onto the grass and sat down on it delightedly—it *was* rather a long way to the ground, and I landed with a bump. The air was overwhelmingly humid, and I could feel the sweat beginning to form under my arms and slide down my sides. I'm going to ruin my dress, I thought, I'm extremely likely to be stinking rather soon, but that quickly turned out to be the least of my worries as a heavy-headed drowsiness seemed to cloud my brain and pull me down farther toward the ground. I began to experience an odd sort of deafness, as if my hearing were slowly being smothered or swallowed in the heaviness of the air, but at the same time the noise of the insects right around me seemed to become suddenly abnormally loud. My dog was running in great circles and sweeps at a distance—it seemed a great distance—and in fact every distance seemed a very great distance. I had no pillow—I put my hand under my head. The earth was very hard, and I could feel the presence all around me of the ants and centipedes and spiders just waiting to crawl up my dress and even inside my face if I should dare to fall asleep. As it seemed unthinkable, I allowed myself to do it. I closed my eyes, thinking sleep was impossible, and within one moment I was fast asleep. *(Pause.)* Not long passed before a strange sensation woke me up. It was my dog at my back, bumping me gently, over and over. A powerful impulse to have intercourse with the dog, a male, made my heart pound rapidly and my face flush hotly with blood, but he, the poor beast, ran away quite suddenly and continued to chase around in circles. The unsatisfied impulse left me quite nervous. I stood up; I felt cold; I drew my raincoat closely around me and walked very fast, with the dog running before me, till we reached the gate and shut it behind us. Twilight was falling. I looked in the windows of shops at dresses. I looked at women's shoes as they passed me on the street. A great wind blew up suddenly—perhaps it would storm. The pavement thronged with huge, big-faced men in suits passing all around me. The sounds of the traffic were incredibly loud. I walked faster and faster, and finally I found myself at the building where Frank lived. I left the dog wandering in the gutter. I entered the building. Inside Frank's apartment, there were already several people there, but Bruce wasn't there yet. Everyone was flirting. I started to drink. The evening went on for quite a little while. I was still feeling nervous. More people kept arriving. There were Steve and Helen and Randy and Dana and Trini. A really great group. I was feeling rather restless. I was feeling rather sick. Bruce finally showed up. "Oh—Am I *late?* Oh, *I'm* sorry, darling—" He looked like a prince. He was handsome. He looked like a god. He talked with several other women. Then he talked with me. He himself began drinking.

BRUCE: Very delicious. I think I'll get plowed. I'm *really* enjoying this party—the people here are great—really fantastic—really delightful—

MARIE: Janet, in particular—eh, darling?—

BRUCE: Janet? Janet? What? Are you joking? Aha ha ha ha! Aha ha ha ha! Janet? Janet? Well, darling, Janet's an unusual woman—I mean, do you know, she's actually a dancer! But really, darling—

MARIE: Well, she's very attractive.

BRUCE: Well yes, I know, well yes, yes she is, but not to *me*, you see, darling! Not to *me*, darling!

MARIE: A little overheated, though, by her, sweetheart?—I mean, you seem over—

BRUCE: What? What? Over-what? Darling, what in the world are you saying?

MARIE: You seem a little—

BRUCE: Eh? What? You must be crackers! Absolutely crackers, darling! I'm as sound as a bell, if you get my meaning— Whoops— ergh—

MARIE: Spilled the drink?—er?—darling?—

BRUCE: Hey—wow! Got to watch the angle of those fucking—those fucking—

MARIE: Bruce—darling—you seem a bit tight— a bit high—

BRUCE: Listen—are you kidding? You're in very good hands tonight, darling, believe me. Believe me, I'm in very good shape. I'm really in *very* good shape. And you're not in such bad shape yourself, you know, darling.

I mean, fuck Janet, *you're* looking *very attractive*. Very very attractive, darling. I'm really not kidding. I mean, you really look great. Your hair, darling, and that marvelous lipstick—

MARIE: Well—Bruce—

BRUCE: No, darling, really. I'm really being serious. The people at this party are very excited by you, darling. I've been watching the way that they're looking you over. I mean, these people would really like to have you, darling. They *really* like to have you. They *really* want you, if you get my meaning.

MARIE: Well—Bruce—

BRUCE: You see, I'm being very serious now, darling. I mean, I want you to know—you have an incredible power over all of these people—

MARIE: Well—Bruce—

BRUCE: Listen—have some of my drink here, darling, I can see that you're thirsty— No really—take it—

MARIE: Darling, I think you're a little bit insane tonight, dear, a little drunk, a little absurd—

BRUCE: Darling, your hands are awfully cold—why is that?

MARIE: I really don't know.

BRUCE: But why are your hands cold, darling? Are you sick? Are you?

MARIE: I don't think so, Bruce.

BRUCE: Listen to me, darling. You don't think it's possible—

MARIE: What? What?

BRUCE: No—darling—

MARIE: Am I sick? Cancer? What? Bruce? Some serious illness? Do you think—

BRUCE: Ha ha ha— *No,* darling, I was referring to the flu— But I mean I'm sure you're all *right,* you just looked a bit *peaked.* But now you just sit here quietly and I'll get you a drink—you need another drink now, darling.

MARIE: What?

BRUCE *exits.*

(To audience) He ran off in the direction of the bar. I was feeling quite hot, quite flushed. There were people who were talking quite near me. I could hear them.

HERB *(to* ENID *and* BETTINA*):* Well, you see, I've worked my ass off, I mean I've really worked my ass off for the guy, I mean for three whole years, with no credit for myself, with no respect being paid to myself, and I've just sat there quietly and listened to people talk about him, and praise him, and say how great he is—"Oh yes, isn't he great, what a marvelous man, he's so extraordinary, he's so remarkable"—and I've just been sitting there day after day just taking it all in—and that's fine, that's wonderful, but the problem happens to be that the guy is really driving me bananas—I mean, the guy is *insane,* he's just fucking *insane,* I mean he keeps coming into my office and just poking at my desk and sort of saying, "Well, *Herb,* how are *things?"* I mean, the guy is *insane,* it's just really impossible, and I've done what I can for the guy, I mean I've helped him, I've worked very hard for the guy for three whole years, I mean I've worked my ass off, but he just can't leave me alone, and it's really just driving me bananas to the point where I really don't know what to do. Do you see what I'm saying?

ENID: Yeah—sure—

HENRY *(to* ANTOINE*):* Excuse me. Excuse me. Let me get *this* part straight in my head before we go any farther. All right? I mean, you seem to be saying that children don't need to learn to read. I mean, isn't that really your point?—because the point that you're making is that reading is really just completely out of date—I mean, it's just not necessary today—we just don't require it— Isn't that what you're saying?

ANTOINE: No.

HENRY: Oh, I'm sorry. I thought that's what you just finished saying—

BRUCE *(returning):* Well, here you go, darling. Here's that drink. And here's one for me. Good *Christ,* I like these. But are you all right, darling? Are you feeling a bit better? I mean, you look just great. You look *great,* darling. Just *great*. *Great*. So why don't you tell me—be frank with me, darling. I mean really, let's really be serious. Let's be absolutely true to what we feel. I mean, really, darling, do you care for me at all? I mean, let's talk frankly. Do you actually like me? What do you feel? Why not *really* tell me. Do you love me, darling? Do you actually love me?

MARIE: Well, Bruce, really—I find you very attractive, if that's what you mean. You're a very beautiful man, Bruce. You're a very beautiful man. You have a very, very beautiful body, actually.

BRUCE: Well, darling, darling—do you *really* find me handsome?

MARIE: You're a very handsome man, Bruce. You're a very, very *attractive* man.

BRUCE: That's very exciting. I *like* that, darling. I really do *like* it. Only—aha ha—you should *fuck* me more often then, darling, if you find me so handsome.

MARIE: Oh Bruce—really—

BRUCE: No, really—I mean it—you should *fuck* me more often—I mean, because you can be sort of a *cunt* at certain times, darling, when you refuse to fuck me—I mean, I'm just saying that you really should *fuck* me more often—

MARIE: I hear you, Bruce—

BRUCE: Well of course I'm being an asshole—I know that, darling. I mean sometimes that's just my way, I mean I seem to be an asshole. I mean, some people aren't, but I just happen to be one somehow—an asshole, I mean —I mean, you know me, darling—

MARIE: Bruce, really—

BRUCE: But I need another drink. I mean, I really do like these drinks here tonight— they're just extremely decently prepared! Shall I get you one, sweetheart? I'll bet you'd like one as well, now wouldn't you? I'll *bet* you would.

He exits.

MARIE: He left me quickly. He didn't return with the drink. I sat on the sofa—the most comfortable in the room. For a long while no one came near me. I sat by myself and did nothing. I stared at the fabric that covered the sofa. Then I noticed a book that was sitting right by me on a table. I started looking at the pictures. There were scenes of waterfalls and rivers and nudes of both sexes and children. They were lying on the grass in the sunlight; their limbs lay open without shame. Then people came nearer; they were sitting right next to me, talking.

ANTOINE *(to* HENRY*)*: No, I really didn't say that children don't need to learn to read, you see. I wasn't talking about that. I just said that there will soon be machines on the market that will be capable of reading books aloud.

HENRY: Yes—so people won't need to read them to themselves—exactly—that's just great. Yes, it seems to me we're talking about a world without any books at all, aren't we? I mean, books will just be out— I mean really—just—no more books!—no more books of any kind— Because they really won't be needed, will they? So why should anyone learn to read? Why should they? I mean, isn't that what the whole situation comes to, really?

ANTOINE: Well, why say there won't be any books? There may very well be books. But machines could read them out loud, or else some books might appear on certain forms of tape that a machine could more easily read.

HENRY: Yes, I see.

HERB *(to* ENID *and* BETTINA*)*: And then, I know this is funny, but actually the most difficult part of the whole *thing* for me is that I just can't help *liking* the guy in a way, I mean he's not a bad guy, he's really all right, I'm actually quite fond of him as a person, you see, but it's just so hard to *deal* with a guy like that on a day-to-day basis, because you're always thinking, Well, I don't want to hurt him, his feelings might be hurt, and it can actually become almost manipulative, really, because you don't want to hurt the guy's feelings, but on the other hand you really want to *do* certain things that would probably really hurt him, and you really *should* do them, but you just don't want to—

ENID: Yeah—yeah—

BETTINA: But you know—I mean—I understand what you're saying, but I mean isn't it possible for people just to sometimes not feel what they actually do feel?

HERB: What?

BETTINA: I mean, they may actually feel a certain thing, but they don't really *know* that they do, because in their own conscious minds they're so incredibly involved in what they *think* that they feel that they really don't feel the thing at all—do you know what I mean? I mean, sometimes a person can have some feeling that they *think* is a feeling of liking some person, but it may actually be some other kind of feeling, but they think that they *ought* to be feeling some kind of affection for that person, and so they think that they feel it when actually what they feel is something completely different—I mean they might feel resentment or even anger toward that person, but they think that they *ought* to feel affection, so they think that they do, but actually they don't.

ENID: You mean—

BETTINA: I mean like for example a very common example is when a person is supposed to feel pleased by something—I mean like when someone gives you a present, and you're supposed to feel pleased, but actually you don't, because the thing is something that actually you hate or you actually already have the thing—well then, you're not supposed to say, "Well I really hate this," you're supposed to say, "Oh *boy,* that's great, I really like it," so then actually you know that you don't actually feel pleased, but you don't want to hurt the person's feelings, so you just kind of say, "Oh wow, that's great, it's just what I wanted—" I mean, this isn't really an example of when you *think* you feel something but you really don't feel it, but it just shows how sometimes you can actually be feeling two completely different feelings at once, because on the one hand you don't like the thing that you got but on the other hand you don't want to hurt the person's feelings, particularly if they're someone you like and they tried to get you something you'd enjoy, but actually it's something that you *hate* or you already have. I mean, there's sometimes a difference, because sometimes a person is actually giving you something that unconsciously they know that you'll hate, but sometimes they just really think that you'll like it but for some particular reason it just happens to turn out that you actually don't.

HERB: I really don't know what you mean, Bettina.

BRUCE *(returning)*: Well, here's that drink now, my love.

MARIE: Thank you, Bruce. I really feel sick.

BRUCE: Well, you just rest right here, darling. You can even fall asleep. No one's going to disturb you.

He exits.

MARIE: I lay back against the sofa. I closed my eyes and listened to everyone talking. Then I fell asleep. I dreamed of pleasurable excursions, a trip to the beach. Bruce and I seemed to find a world in which every person was somehow extremely complex and interesting, but at the same time terribly relaxed. These people in the dream each had their own apartments, their own tastes. We were always going over for dinner at their houses. One person served a kind of soft fried noodles, with pea pods and peas.

JEAN *(to* TIM*)*: You can see these things from different points of view, you see, Tim. You can see them a little bit differently from the way *you* see them. Some people don't have a lot of money, you know.

TIM: Well Jean, I know that.

JEAN: Some people can't afford to buy a piano. Did you ever think of that? Some people can't afford to buy a *guitar*. They can't *have* musical soirées. They can't *sing* madrigals in the evenings and put on performances—did you ever think of that? Maybe they're just a little bit too tired, from *working*. Maybe they're just a little bit too *hungry*, if it's not too embarrassing to say that—"Oh, *now* she's *really* exaggerating—*too hungry —how absurd—*" Well it may not be so absurd, as a matter of fact. It may not be so incredibly absurd!

FRED *(to* ILSA*)*: And *obviously* I'm not saying that I know the whole story. I'm not saying that I know more than you do. I've been there, of course, but I've never really lived there. I don't really know about the way things work there. I've read certain articles—

ILSA: You've written—?—

FRED: I say I've *read* certain articles—I've read certain articles, I've talked to some of the people who know more than I do— And the fact happens to be that I just *happened* to be there at a very odd moment, and I happened to be there when some of the things that I've read about just *happened* to be occurring—

JEAN *(to* TIM*)*: Listen, there are babies out there who are dying because they were brought up on milk that was intentionally mislabeled—I mean, milk that was *mixed with water*—

TIM: But Jean—

JEAN: There are old men and old women—I mean, these people could have been our parents—and they can't afford to buy *underwear*—I mean, these are people with pride, it makes them actually *ashamed,* but they need all the money that they have just to survive and pay the rent—

TIM: I know—

JEAN: I mean, maybe *they'd* like to sing madrigals. Maybe *they'd* like to sing madrigals. But they don't have anything to wear!

MARIE: Then I dreamt we had a house, with chickens and snakes on the grass outside, and broken eggshells, and I dreamt we went to a restaurant, with beautiful tablecloths and napkins, and Bruce was holding my hand at the table, and then it was a long summer night, and we were making love over and over again.

FRED *(to* ILSA*)*: I mean, I saw that man being pressed between two panes of glass—and it was horrible, horrible—I mean, you just can't imagine—the way his tongue was hanging to one side—he looked just like a slaughtered *beast*—

ILSA: But why are you telling me this?

FRED: I said that *these* are the articles— *These* people are— Don't you see—*that's* what I was trying to explain to your brother—

ILSA: Well don't bring *him* into this—

FRED: Don't what?—

ILSA: Don't bring—

FRED: But he's *already* in it. He's *already* in it. He *is* involved in this. He *is* involved in it. *He's* in the field we're discussing. Don't tell me not to *bring* him into it. He *is* in it.

ILSA: I really don't feel like talking about this. I really don't want to.

HENRY *(to* ANTOINE*)*: So is that why you think that children should listen to popular music in school? Because when you have these—machines?—

ANTOINE: Well, you're really distorting my—

HENRY: Well, what am I distorting? I mean, isn't that just what you said? That children should listen to popular music in school? Didn't you say that? Or maybe I didn't quite follow you, somehow.

ANTOINE: Well, you're drawing a connection between two such completely different things. I mean, the fact that these machines have been invented really doesn't have much to do with my opinions about popular music.

HENRY: Well, are you trying to get away from what you said? I mean, first you said that they didn't need to learn how to read, and then you talked about listening to popular music. That's what *I* understood. I mean, didn't you talk about listening to popular music? That children would be listening to popular music in school?

ANTOINE: Well, I mentioned certain forms of music, yes. But—er—really—why are you so upset by the thought of popular music? I mean, why do you think it bothers you so much?

HENRY: It doesn't bother me a bit.

ANTOINE: Well, don't you think there's anything to be learned from listening to it, then?

HENRY: I'm not saying there isn't.

ANTOINE: Well then what *are* you saying?

HENRY: I'm just saying— Well—ha! aha ha!—I just happen to have these very odd opinions, I'm afraid—you see, I just *happen* to believe in certain values— Well—to *me,* you see, when you see that children are living in a certain way—I mean, let's not be absurd—I mean, really—let's face it—how can I describe it?—when you see that children are eating when they like, sleeping when they like—

ANTOINE: Well, you misunderstand me if you think I'm encouraging some form of—er—chaos—

HENRY: Well, I see, I *see*—so that goes too far even for you, does it? Eating when they like? Sleeping when they like? That's *very* interesting. I'm *very* interested in your reaction to that—

BRUCE *(to audience)*: Well, I had another drink at the bar, and then I bumped into a girl named Susie, and we talked for a while, and then she moved along, and then I just sat by myself just thinking about my day. I'd had quite a day! First, lunch with Roger. That was enjoyable as always. And then I had some shopping to do, and I went on a big expedition to the farthest end of the city—you can get some incredible bargains out there—and when I'd finished my shopping,

I decided to walk more or less in the direction of Frank's through some unknown sections of town. And I just walked through all sorts of sections. I even found a place where there were fishermen mending their boats, and little fish were flopping all about, and sails were flapping, and you could actually smell water and seaweed. And then there was another place not far along from that one—it was a marvelous park, with stiff pointed trees just clumped all together and very dark green, and I wandered around in it for an hour or so. And then finally I got thirsty, and I looked for this wonderful café that I'd been to years before where they made this drink made of freshly squeezed orange juice and soda. And after quite a lot of looking, I finally found it, and I went inside and sat down at the counter. I was sipping my drink when a tanned young woman came in wearing shorts and a light-colored, lightweight shirt, without a brassiere. If you looked at her closely, her nipples could actually be seen through the shirt. She sat down right next to me and ordered some food, and then she started reading this big sheet of newspaper that she'd carried in with her. Her hands weren't clean, and the paper looked ripped, as if she'd torn it from some old pile of

trash. And then the material in the paper—
I could easily read it—was of a kind that
really could have been of no interest at all
to this girl, but she seemed to be reading it
with total absorption as if nothing else mattered. Then the waitress brought along a
glass of water and placed it beside her. Still
reading the paper, the girl put her hand out
and tried to reach for the glass, but she
missed. Then she looked up and ever so
gently took the glass with both hands and
lifted it to her lips and drank from it slowly
and carefully, as if it were valuable wine.
"Good," I thought to myself, "A nut. A
maniac. My type of girl." I could easily pick
her up. I could easily get her, I thought. I
was leaning way over, straining so hard to
see the nipples through her shirt— Forget
it, those nipples can wait, I thought; if I'm
actually going to fuck her, I can look at any
part of her I like. I mean, if I'm going to be
fucking this girl, I'm not going to be fucking
her while she's wearing her clothes! Just
then, the waitress brought her food. I stared
at her plate. Suddenly she speared an enormous piece of meat on her fork and was
about to stick it in her mouth. "Wait!" I said.
"That meat is hot!" She looked at me,
amazed. She took a small bite of the meat.
We sat there next to each other, neither of

us speaking. Then she turned away from me and addressed herself totally to her meal. My face felt hot. She was eating incredibly slowly, making very strange movements with her lips. I looked at her legs. They were heavy. If I fucked this girl, she might go mad while being fucked—after all, she was insane! I decided to masturbate instead. I walked to a hotel, checked in, and went upstairs to a room. I immediately looked out the window to see if there were windows across the way. There were. In one of them, a woman seemed to be cleaning her apartment. I sat down in a chair near the window. I forgot about masturbating, and I watched the woman, hoping that something would happen. She was pretty good-looking, she was tall and thin. After fifteen minutes, impulsively, she pulled off her shirt, and her breasts were totally revealed. I couldn't believe what had happened. My head felt light. I was trembling. She stood in the window for a moment, as if wondering what to do. Then she left the room. I sat frozen in my chair. My eyes held on to the window like a carpenter's vise holding on to a big piece of wood, but nothing seemed to happen. After an interval that seemed like about an hour or an hour and a half, I finally shifted my position in my chair, and a little after that, the woman came back. She was wearing a bathrobe. She sat down on a sofa. I watched her while she sat there and read. I thought she would take off the bathrobe. She would have to take it off in order to get dressed for the evening. A long time passed. Then she stood up and pulled down the shade. There was a tiny crack between the shade and the sill. I could see a bit of her bathrobe; her hands were untying the cord. Then she moved away, and came back in some kind of a dress. Then the lights in her apartment went out, and the window was black. Sweat was pouring down my face. It was late— I was sitting in darkness. A telephone rang somewhere down the hall. I jumped. I stood up. I ran out of the room. I looked at my watch—I was already due there at Frank's. I left the hotel and went out into the evening. I started to run, but I didn't want to run too fast—I was afraid of sweating. I walked with big strides, rapidly, controlling the sweat. The air was greasy. I made it to Frank's just a little bit late.

HERB *(to* ROXANNE*)*: You see, please don't misunderstand me, I'm not trying to say that the guy isn't nice. I don't mean that at all. The truth is that I actually like him. He happens to be just a very nice guy. The only problem is, he just drives me bananas—do you know what I mean?

ROXANNE: Oh God—yeah—I know—I know—

MARIE *(to audience)*: I slept so soundly. My body seemed to sink into the sofa so heavily, so far, like an object falling in water. When I woke up again, I felt really sick. Bruce was sitting right next to me, talking.

BRUCE *(to MARIE)*: Well, darling, I'm glad you're waking up. You had me worried for a while. I was just having a conversation with some people over there, and you know, there are some interesting things about the treatment of certain illnesses that *Jack* was explaining to me. Do you know—?—there was a time when vomiting was induced in patients whom today we would classify as mentally ill. Then the vomit itself would be kept in containers, because usually the simple reappearance of one of these containers would be sufficient in itself to lead the patient into another fit of vomiting.

Pause.

MARIE: Bruce—did you slap me while I was sleeping?

BRUCE: Why—of course not, darling! What do you mean? Are you crazy?

MARIE: I don't feel normal.

BRUCE: God—darling—you don't think you might be mentally ill now, do you? I mean, darling, you don't think you might be crazy, do you? I mean, do you think you might actually be crazy now? God, darling, I really hope not—

MARIE: Bruce—help me—

BRUCE: I've had this terrible feeling lately that something was about to happen to you, darling—

MARIE: Just talk to me, Bruce. Help me. Hold me.

BRUCE: God, let me see. Do I have anything to tell you? Well, Roger and I had a *marvelous* lunch—prawns with peas—it was absolutely great.

MARIE: Darling—I'm sick—

BRUCE: Er—and then—oh, yes! Gloria and I were just having the most fascinating conversation. You know, we were talking about the whole *question* of people having *servants!*—have you ever *thought* about that? I mean, it's just such a fascinating subject—and I was sort of saying that it really seems to me sort of a shame that the whole tradition of people having servants has just gone out of style, because really the whole point of having servants was actually that servants were people who could be counted on to care about your welfare, and even sort of respect you, whether you *deserved* it or *not*, and I really *like* that, I just think it's such a nice thing. And I mean I was even saying that personally I wouldn't particularly have minded being a servant myself—I mean, it wasn't such a bad occupation! I mean, it must have been rather nice to work in a home rather than an office or a factory, and the food must have been pretty good as well—I mean, you could eat whatever the family ate, or else you could go into the kitchen and fix whatever you liked for yourself—Oh, but, darling, I've *bored* you! Oh, *darling*, I'm *sorry!* Oh really, how dreadful—

MARIE: Bruce—

BRUCE: Oh God, I'm so *awful.* I'm just *so awful,* darling. What a boring person—

MARIE: Bruce—

BRUCE: No, *really,* I'm sorry. I'm just doing you no good at all. Anyway, I'm going to go over by the bar again now, darling. I'll get you another drink, and meanwhile you can just keep resting. I've got to have a word with Grace over there.

MARIE: With who, Bruce?

BRUCE: You remember her, darling—that friend of Chuck?—that brunette?—the one who went fishing in her panties?—

MARIE What?

BRUCE: Ha—actually—ha ha—I spent the night with her once about eleven years ago. I'll tell you, she was really amazing. I'll never forget—ha—pardon me, darling, but her vagina was just incredibly tight, you know? It was just like being gripped by a hand. I mean, I remember, by the time we were finished, my penis was absolutely *bright red* —I mean, it looked just like a raw piece of meat, or fish—and I just felt absolutely drained—I mean, my testicles were really just as dry as bones—they ached for a week — Oh *God,* it was great—it was really something—

MARIE: Darling—I'm sick—

BRUCE: Darling, why is it that whenever we have a conversation you always feel sick? You ask me to talk to you, and then when I do you feel sick. Have you ever really noticed that, darling? It's really a pattern with you. It's sort of upsetting. And it actually gives me a pain in the ass, if you really want to know.

MARIE: All right, Bruce.

BRUCE: And I mean, really, darling, the expressions you get on your face sometimes—I mean, these people are going to think you're an absolute nut—

MARIE: I said all right, Bruce. All right. All right.

BRUCE *exits.*

He talked with the woman he'd described. I went to Frank's bedroom to get my raincoat. A woman named Selena was living with Frank; his bedroom was crammed with all of her things. There were bottles and creams and combs and lotions. The tables held vases that held white flowers. The only light was from a little toy lamp that was sitting by the phone. I sat by the lamp in a little toy chair, catching my breath after searching through the closet, through her clothes and his clothes, till I found my coat. A powerful smell of urine seeped through the window. It passed over my lips. It mingled with the smell of perfume in the room. My hand was playing with a huge fur coat on the bed. I closed my eyes, and I thought I was praying, but that my prayers were falling on deaf ears, which was the phrase that I thought of. Then the telephone rang. I got up to answer it. I thought it would be a murderer. I thought it would be a person who was coming to kill me. I thought it would be a torturer who was coming to strip me and strap me down and beat me with his fists and then rape me. I thought it would be thick poison gas pouring into my mouth over the phone. But no—it was just a friend of Frank named Willy. I heard his tiny voice through the receiver. I went to find Frank. I went to find Bruce. I was feeling very sick. We left the party, and we walked to a restaurant. I picked it; I like it. I used to go there all the time when I was single. I used to go there by myself. I used to eat there by myself. It was down at the end of a street near a pier. It was a pretty long walk, but I felt like walking. It was almost raining. Unbelievably attractive men kept passing us and smiling. We ate dinner in silence. The restaurant was cold.

Long silence. Three or four pots of espresso coffee, and extra cups, are on the table in front of MARIE. BRUCE *is eating.* MARIE *sips coffee. The* WAITER *approaches them, bringing another pot of coffee.*

WAITER: Well—er—here's your coffee. Shall I clear away these other cups and pots?—eheh—

MARIE: Yes, why don't you? Thank you.

Very long silence. The WAITER *clears away the cups and pots and exits.* BRUCE *eats.* MARIE *sips coffee.*

BRUCE: Er— Darling, you seem to be drinking a lot of coffee, sweetheart—do you think that's wise? *(Silence. She sips coffee.)* I mean—I—er—wonder, darling— *(Silence)* I mean, sometimes it makes you a bit nervous—er—don't you think so?

MARIE: What? What? Are you telling me something?

BRUCE: Well, *you* know, darling, I was really just talking. I mean, you know me, darling—sometimes I say things— *(Silence)* No—I mean, darling, I was only saying that sometimes—I mean, you seem a little bit nervous already tonight, darling—I mean, I seem to detect this—and I sometimes notice that sometimes when actually you already *are* feeling nervous, you seem to like to drink coffee, but sometimes that can actually have the effect of actually making you *more* nervous than you already were before—so that's really all I was trying to say, actually, darling. That's all. I'm sorry. I didn't mean to upset you.

Silence.

MARIE: Do you know that I never loved you, Bruce? I never loved you. I never loved you.

BRUCE: Ah. Yes—

MARIE: You see, I *never* loved you. That's really the truth. I *never* loved you. I pretended to you; I hardly even pretended to myself. *(Silence.)* You see—I don't even like you. No—not at all. I don't like you. I don't respect you. You're nothing but shit as far as I'm concerned.

Silence.

BRUCE: Darling, do you think we should just have our dinner for the moment? I mean, perhaps we should go into all this when we've finished our meal.

MARIE: I don't enjoy your company. I don't enjoy being with you. You're pitiful, you're pathetic, and you're actually one of the least interesting people I've ever met in my life.

BRUCE: Yes—well—my darling, what do you think?—are we going to have our meal here or not? I mean, this was the restaurant that *you* wanted to go to, and personally I would rather have had something cheap, and this is *not* my favorite kind of food, but if we're going to be here, it seems somewhat absurd if all we're going to do is just have an unpleasant conversation.

MARIE: Bruce—

BRUCE: I mean, I had thought we would have a nice evening together. I know you're unhappy. But we could discuss your unhappiness and still have a very nice evening together.

MARIE: I hate you, Bruce. That's why I have to leave you. I'm very, very sorry.

Very long silence. They move slightly in their chairs. Silence.

BRUCE: Yes, you know the amazing thing, darling?—I really *like* these homosexuals, these "homos." I mean, really, they're great! Jack for example. He's a fabulous fellow—really. A *marvelous* person. *(Silence.)* I mean, he's just terribly agreeable, he's *nice* in other words, I mean, he knows how to make people relax, feel good. *(Pause.)* Now Edwina was *extremely* upset, for example. He calmed her right down. I mean, somehow, he has some special quality that most of us just lack. He knows how to make people relax! *(Pause.)* Well, darling, you know I won't disturb you. I won't keep talking. I know you'd rather have me be quiet. I know how you feel. I was trying to talk, but

I can see that it's better to be quiet. It's all right, darling. I'm just going to sit here, and we'll just be quiet, and we can finish our meal.

Silence. BERT *and* ED *enter and sit at the next table.* BRUCE *and* MARIE *try to eat as* BERT *and* ED *talk. They can hear* BERT *and* ED*'s conversation.*

BERT *(to* ED*)*: It was an extraordinary thing—because I'd been feeling worse and worse for several days. I mean, I'd feel just fine, and then I'd eat, and I'd have this sensation that somehow the food was just rotting in my stomach. I mean, something wasn't happening correctly in there. And then I'd suddenly get these sharp, shooting pains, like a sort of a flash, like lightning, through the entire length of my asshole somehow—you know? And then by Friday afternoon there was this whole new sensation—my stomach started giving these little leaps—these lurches—like this—bip! bip!—and I would feel like going to the bathroom really badly, but then in about two seconds the sensation would go away, and I'd feel all right again, and I wouldn't feel like going to the bathroom anymore. Well finally, late in the afternoon, I felt one of these *lurches*—but instead of going away, it just sort of took a hold on my gut—it just sort of *stayed* there, and so I sort of really *rushed* into the bathroom, and I sat down on the toilet, and then right then all of a sudden I really began to feel dizzy and faint—it was really awful. I thought I was going to throw up, but I didn't, but I sort of began to see spots in front of my eyes—my vision got cloudy. And I was shitting and shitting, but it was terribly painful. Anyway, finally I finished, and I slowly stood up—and I remember, when I stood up, I almost fell over—the floor seemed to be rising to meet me—and I was leaning against the wall, and then I was about to flush the toilet, and it occurred to me to look at my stool. Well you can imagine how I felt—I looked down at the stool, and it was covered with *blood.*

ED: My God—how awful—

BRUCE *has approached them.*

BRUCE: Excuse me. I'm sorry. Er—excuse me—you see—er—we're eating our meal—

BERT: You what?

BRUCE: I say, we're eating our meal, and your—conversation—we couldn't help hearing—

BERT: What? What?

BRUCE: We can't—er—we're eating—argh—

BERT *(to* ED*)*: Is this guy trying to tell me I'm talking too loudly?

BRUCE: Well, sir—er—

ED *(to* BRUCE*)*: Pardon me. Can I make a suggestion? Would you mind? I'd like you to return to your table. That way we won't have any kind of trouble.

BRUCE: Oh—I see—yes. Oh yes, well if that's the way you feel, well then yes—I see—uh-huh—all right. Fine. Fine. Well, all right—yes—oh yes—uh-huh—

He returns to his place. Pause.

MARIE: You eat shit, Bruce. You're a worthless turd.

BRUCE: Yes—well—okay, okay—

MARIE: I'm sorry I met you. I'm sorry I knew you. Of all the men I ever knew, you turn out to be the worst. And the incredible thing is that I never loved you.

BRUCE: Well—I thought you did.

MARIE: But you see, you were wrong. It's very, very sad. Our dinner is spoiled, and my life was spoiled, because I met you. I wish I hadn't. I wish I hadn't.

BRUCE: Yeah—it's a shame—

MARIE: You horrible shit—

BRUCE: Yeah—that's right—

MARIE: You horrible shit.

BRUCE: Would you like to go now, darling? I don't imagine you'll be wanting dessert—er—

MARIE: No?

BRUCE: Well, I didn't—

MARIE: Well fuck you, Bruce. Maybe I'd like some.

BRUCE: Oh well, great. That's great. Let's have some—yes! Ah—sir?

WAITER *(entering)*: Yes?

BRUCE: We'll have that thing with pears right now, actually.

WAITER: Oh—all right.

BRUCE: Yes, that would be great.

   WAITER *exits.*

MARIE: "Yes, that would be great."

BRUCE: Darling, must you always mock me?

MARIE: Well, Bruce, I'm afraid I can't help it. You're just so mockable. You're my mockable boy. *(Long silence.)* But, Bruce, really—do you actually not care at all that I'm leaving you?

BRUCE: Oh—are you leaving me, darling?

MARIE: Yes, Bruce, I'm planning to leave you.

BRUCE: Well, darling—you know you shouldn't leave me, I mean, you know you shouldn't leave me—

MARIE: Well, Bruce, I'm planning to leave you.

BRUCE: Oh. Well. Well, darling, it's a little funny just to tell me this, isn't it? I mean, what brings this up just at the moment, you see—I mean, what have I done? We've just gone to a certain restaurant for dinner, and I'd understood it to be one that you liked. And as far as I can tell, it's lived up to expectation at *least* one hundred percent, I would say.

MARIE: Oh, Bruce—you're funny. You really are. *(Pause.)* So you don't actually care that I'm leaving you, then?

BRUCE: Well, you're really not *leaving* me, darling, I mean, you feel you would *like* to, but you really aren't actually leaving, if you see what I mean.

MARIE: You don't think I'm leaving?

BRUCE: Well—are you?

MARIE: Yes—I am, Bruce. I really am.

BRUCE: Well, darling, I mean, you know you can't leave me. I mean, don't you know that I love you, darling? I mean, really, after all—er—

MARIE: "Love" me? You "love" me? Bruce—you don't even know the meaning of the word. You don't know the meaning of the word, Bruce.

BRUCE: Oh—really? I always thought I did. How very very strange—

MARIE: Bruce—don't you know that you're not a living person?

Silence.

BRUCE: I'm sorry, darling. I thought I was one.

Silence. The WAITER *brings the dessert and exits.*

But what am I, then? I run around like a living person. I say things, I talk to people, I even have certain feelings, believe it or not.

MARIE: Bruce, I can't talk. I don't feel well. I feel very dizzy.

BRUCE: I *try* to be decent—

MARIE: Shut up, Bruce.

BRUCE: I mean, I try very hard to be—

MARIE: Please, Bruce. Please be quiet. Please be quiet, Bruce. I really don't feel well. I really don't feel well.

BRUCE: I'm sorry, darling.

Silence.

MARIE: You see, you're *not* human, you're *not* a person, you *have* no connection to me, or to any other person, and you never will have one, and you never can have one, and that's why to me you are nothing but a filthy piece of shit that is attached to me physically, but now I am cutting you off of me, you see. I am cutting you off of me, I am cutting you away from me.

BRUCE: Marie—

MARIE: No—you see, Bruce, you see, Bruce, you're *not alive.* You're *not* a *person.* You are *not* a *person,* you are only *meat.* I am telling you the truth now, Bruce, and I'm telling you that you are *dead*. You're a horrible dead piece of *meat*.

BRUCE: Marie—

MARIE: No—shut up! Shut up! I am calling you dead. I am pronouncing you dead. As far as I'm concerned, you are now *dead*. You are now nothing. Your face is nothing. Your expressions are nothing. Your face is a behind. You are now filth. You are only filth. Your face is *not* a face. Your expressions are *not* expressions. And so because you are now nothing and you are now dead, it means nothing to me to leave you, because you are now nothing. You are death. And I don't know anything about you, because you are meat. You are only meat. God help me—I know what it means to be sitting with nothing. You may say things, but I don't have to listen, because you are death. You are filth. You are only meat. You are filth. You are only filth.

Silence.

BRUCE: Darling?

MARIE: What?

BRUCE: Darling—do you know what I did today? I bought a new typewriter for myself. And you know—it really wasn't expensive. I mean, I got it on sale, and it was incredibly cheap. I tried it out in the store, and it worked like a charm. I mean—I really loved it! And they were even willing to deliver it for free. They're bringing it tomorrow.

Pause.

MARIE: Will you miss your old one, Bruce?

BRUCE: Well, you know, I really don't think so.

Silence.

MARIE *(to audience)*: We sat at the table. We finished our dessert. And then I took him home. By the time we left the restaurant, he was drunk once again. He was tired, he was sleepy. We went in a taxi. As we rode, he hugged me tightly. He hugged me as we went around the corners. He hugged me when the taxi went faster. We got home. Our apartment was cool, there was a breeze. I got the clean sheets out of the closet. I made some hot milk. We sat in our chairs and we drank it. Then I put him to bed. I stayed up for a while. I drank some more milk. I read a magazine, a paper. Then I went to bed myself. It was warm under the sheet. I watched the shadows moving on the ceiling. I listened to the cars rushing by outside the window. Then it started to rain. Then it rained and rained. It began very gently, very lightly; then the sound of the rain grew stronger and heavier, and I sank down farther into the darkness of my pillow, and my face went down into the pillow, and my mouth opened wide, and I drooled into the pillow, and I sank down farther into it, and farther, and farther, and I slept.

OTHER GROVE PRESS DRAMA AND THEATER PAPERBACKS

E487 ABE, KOBO / Friends / $2.45
B415 ARDEN, JOHN / John Arden Plays: One (Serjeant Musgrave's Dance, The Workhouse Donkey, Armstrong's Last Goodnight) / $4.95
E610 ARRABAL, FERNANDO / And They Put Handcuffs on the Flowers / $1.95
E611 ARRABAL, FERNANDO / Garden of Delights / $2.95
E521 ARRABAL, FERNANDO / Guernica and Other Plays (The Labyrinth, The Tricycle, Picnic on the Battlefield) / $4.95
E532 ARTAUD, ANTONIN / The Cenci / $3.95
B423 AYCKBOURN, ALAN / Absurd Person Singular, Absent Friends, Bedroom Farce: Three Plays / $3.95
E425 BARAKA, IMAMU AMIRI (LeRoi Jones) / The Baptism and The Toilet: Two Plays / $3.95 [See also Grove Press Modern Drama, John Lahr, ed., E633 / $5.95]
E670 BARAKA, IMAMU AMIRI (LeRoi Jones) / The System of Dante's Hell, The Dead Lecturer and Tales / $4.95
E471 BECKETT, SAMUEL / Cascando and Other Short Dramatic Pieces (Words and Music, Eh Joe, Play, Come and Go, Film) / $3.95
BECKETT, SAMUEL / The Collected Works of Samuel Beckett in Twenty-two Volumes / $85.00
E96 BECKETT, SAMUEL / Endgame / $1.95
E680 BECKETT, SAMUEL / Ends and Odds / $1.95
E502 BECKETT, SAMUEL / Film, A Film Script / $1.95
E623 BECKETT, SAMUEL / First Love and Other Shorts / $1.95
E318 BECKETT, SAMUEL / Happy Days / $2.95
E692 BECKETT, SAMUEL / I Can't Go On; I'll Go On / $6.95
E226 BECKETT, SAMUEL / Krapp's Last Tape and Other Dramatic Pieces (All That Fall, Embers [a Play for Radio], Acts Without Words I and II [mimes]) / $3.95
E33 BECKETT, SAMUEL / Waiting for Godot / $1.95
B411 BEHAN, BRENDAN / The Complete Plays (The Hostage, The Quare Fellow, Richard's Cork Leg, Three One Act Plays for Radio) / $4.95

B60	BRECHT, BERTOLT / Baal, A Man's A Man, The Elephant Calf / $1.95 [See also Seven Plays by Bertolt Brecht, GP248 / $12.50 and The Jewish Wife and Other Short Plays, B80 / $1.95]
B312	BRECHT, BERTOLT / The Caucasian Chalk Circle / $1.95
B119	BRECHT, BERTOLT / Edward II: A Chronicle Play / $1.45
B120	BRECHT, BERTOLT / Galileo / $1.95 [See also Seven Plays by Bertolt Brecht, GP248 / $12.50]
B117	BRECHT, BERTOLT / The Good Woman of Setzuan / $1.95 [See also Seven Plays by Bertolt Brecht, GP248 / $12.50]
B80	BRECHT, BERTOLT / The Jewish Wife and Other Short Plays (In Search of Justice, The Informer, The Elephant Calf, The Measures Taken, The Exception and the Rule, Salzburg Dance of Death) / $1.95
B89	BRECHT, BERTOLT / The Jungle of Cities and Other Plays (Drums in the Night, Roundheads and Peakheads) / $3.95
B129	BRECHT, BERTOLT / Manual of Piety / $2.45
B414	BRECHT, BERTOLT / The Mother / $2.95
B108	BRECHT, BERTOLT / Mother Courage and Her Children / $1.95 [See also Seven Plays by Bertolt Brecht, GP248 / $12.50]
GP248	BRECHT, BERTOLT / Seven Plays by Bertolt Brecht (In the Swamp, A Man's A Man, Saint Joan of the Stockyards, Mother Courage and Her Children, Galileo, The Good Woman of Setzuan, The Caucasian Chalk Circle) / $12.50
B333	BRECHT, BERTOLT / The Threepenny Opera / $1.95
B193	BULGAKOV, MIKHAIL / Heart of a Dog / $2.95
B147	BULGAKOV, MIKHAIL / The Master and Margarita / $3.95
E773	CLURMAN, HAROLD / Nine Plays of the Modern Theater (Waiting for Godot by Samuel Beckett, The Visit by Friedrich Dürrenmatt, Tango by Slawomir Mrozek, The Caucasian Chalk Circle by Bertolt Brecht, The Balcony by Jean Genet, Rhinoceros by Eugène Ionesco, American Buffalo by David Mamet, The Birthday Party by Harold Pinter, and Rosencrantz and Guildenstern Are Dead by Tom Stoppard) / $9.50
E742	COWARD, NOEL / Three Plays (Private Lives, Hay Fever, Blithe Spirit) / $4.50

E159	DELANEY, SHELAGH / A Taste of Honey / $2.95
E34	DURRENMATT, FRIEDRICH / The Visit / $2.95
E130	GENET, JEAN / The Balcony / $2.95
E208	GENET, JEAN / The Blacks: A Clown Show / $3.95 [See also Grove Press Modern Drama, John Lahr, ed., E633 / $5.95]
E577	GENET, JEAN / The Maids and Deathwatch: Two Plays / $3.95
E374	GENET, JEAN / The Screens / $4.95
E677	GRIFFITHS, TREVOR / The Comedians / $3.95
E615	HARRISON, PAUL CARTER, ed. / Kuntu Drama (Great Goodness of Life by Imamu Amiri Baraka, Devil Mas' by Lennox Brown, A Season in the Congo by Aimé Césaire, Mars by Clay Goss, The Great MacDaddy by Paul Carter Harrison, The Owl Answers and A Beast Story by Adrienne Kennedy, Kabnis by Jean Toomer) / $4.95
E457	HERBERT, JOHN / Fortune and Men's Eyes / $4.95
B154	HOCHHUTH, ROLF / The Deputy / $3.95
B417	INGE, WILLIAM / Four Plays by William Inge (Come Back, Little Sheba; Picnic; Bus Stop; The Dark at the Top of the Stairs) / $3.95
E456	IONESCO, EUGENE / Exit the King / $2.95
E101	IONESCO, EUGENE / Four Plays (The Bald Soprano, The Lesson, The Chairs, Jack, or The Submission) / $2.95 [See also One Act: Eleven Short Plays of the Modern Theater, Samuel Moon, ed., B107 / $3.95]
E646	IONESCO, EUGENE / A Hell of a Mess / $3.95
E506	IONESCO, EUGENE / Hunger and Thirst and Other Plays (The Picture, Anger, Salutations) / $3.95
E189	IONESCO, EUGENE / The Killer and Other Plays (Improvisation, or The Shepherd's Chameleon, Maid to Marry) / $3.95
E614	IONESCO, EUGENE / Macbett / $2.95
E589	IONESCO, EUGENE / Present Past, Past Present / $1.95

E259	IONESCO, EUGENE / Rhinoceros and Other Plays (The Leader, The Future Is in Eggs) / $2.95
E485	IONESCO, EUGENE / A Stroll in the Air and Frenzy for Two or More: Two Plays / $2.45
E496	JARRY, ALFRED / The Ubu Plays (Ubu Rex, Ubu Cuckolded, Ubu Enchained) / $3.95
E633	LAHR, JOHN, ed. / Grove Press Modern Drama (The Toilet by Imamu Amiri Baraka [LeRoi Jones], The Caucasian Chalk Circle by Bertolt Brecht, The White House Murder Case by Jules Feiffer, The Blacks by Jean Genet, Rhinoceros by Eugene Ionesco, Tango by Slawomir Mrozek) / $5.95
E668	LION, EUGENE and BALL, DAVID, eds. / Guthrie New Theater, Vol. I (Swellfoot's Tears by Leon Katz, The Future Pit by Menzies McKillop, Cold by Michael Casale, Glutt and Taps by Gladden Schrock, Afternoon Tea by Harvey Perr, Waterman by Frank B. Ford) / $4.95
E697	MAMET, DAVID / American Buffalo / $3.95
E709	MAMET, DAVID / A Life in the Theatre / $3.95
E728	MAMET, DAVID / Reunion and Dark Pony: Two Plays / $2.95
E712	MAMET, DAVID / Sexual Perversity in Chicago and The Duck Variations: Two Plays / $3.95
E716	MAMET, DAVID / The Water Engine and Mr. Happiness: Two Plays / $3.95
B107	MOON, SAMUEL, ed. / One Act: Eleven Short Plays of the Modern Theater (Miss Julie by August Strindberg, Purgatory by William Butler Yeats, The Man With the Flower in His Mouth by Luigi Pirandello, Pullman Car Hiawatha by Thornton Wilder, Hello Out There by William Saroyan, 27 Wagons Full of Cotton by Tennessee Williams, Bedtime Story by Sean O'Casey, Cecile by Jean Anouilh, This Music Crept By Me Upon the Waters by Archibald MacLeish, A Memory of Two Mondays by Arthur Miller, The Chairs by Eugene Ionesco) / $3.95
E433	MROZEK, SLAWOMIR / Tango / $3.95 [See also Grove Press Modern Drama, John Lahr, ed., E633 / $5.95]
E568	MROZEK, SLAWOMIR / Vatzlav / $1.95

E650	NICHOLS, PETER / The National Health / $3.95
B429	ODETS, CLIFFORD / Six Plays of Clifford Odets (Waiting for Lefty, Awake and Sing, Golden Boy, Rocket to the Moon, Till the Day I Die, Paradise Lost) / $5.95
B400	ORTON, JOE / The Complete Plays (The Ruffian on the Stair, The Good and Faithful Servant, The Erpingham Camp, Funeral Games, Loot, What the Butler Saw, Entertaining Mr. Sloane) / $4.95
E724	PINTER, HAROLD / Betrayal / $3.95
E315	PINTER, HAROLD / The Birthday and The Room: Two Plays / $2.95
E299	PINTER, HAROLD / The Caretaker and The Dumb Waiter: Two Plays / $2.95
B402	PINTER, HAROLD / Complete Works: One (The Birthday Party, The Room, The Dumb Waiter, A Slight Ache, A Night Out, The Black and White, The Examination) / $3.95
B403	PINTER, HAROLD / Complete Works: Two (The Caretaker, Night School, The Dwarfs, The Collection, The Lover, Five Revue Sketches) / $3.95
B410	PINTER, HAROLD / Complete Works: Three (Landscape, Silence, The Basement, Six Revue Sketches, Tea Party [play], Tea Party [short story], Mac) / $3.95
E411	PINTER, HAROLD / The Homecoming / $2.45
E555	PINTER, HAROLD / Landscape and Silence: Two Plays / $3.95 [See also Complete Works: Three by Harold Pinter, B410 / $3.95]
GP604	PINTER, HAROLD / Mac (A Memoir) / $4.50 [See also Complete Works: Three by Harold Pinter, B410 / $3.95]
E663	PINTER, HAROLD / No Man's Land / $1.95
E606	PINTER, HAROLD / Old Times / $1.95
E350	PINTER, HAROLD / Three Plays (The Collection, A Slight Ache, The Dwarfs) / $4.95 [See also Complete Works: One by Harold Pinter, B402 / $3.95 and Complete Works: Two by Harold Pinter, B403 / $3.95]

E744	POMERANCE, BERNARD / The Elephant Man / $2.95
E497	SHAW, ROBERT / The Man in the Glass Booth / $2.95
E686	STOPPARD, TOM / Albert's Bridge and Other Plays (If You're Glad I'll Be Frank, Artist Descending a Staircase, Where Are They Now? A Separate Peace) / $3.95
E684	STOPPARD, TOM / Dirty Linen and New-Found-Land: Two Plays / $2.95
E703	STOPPARD, TOM / Every Good Boy Deserves Favor and The Professional Foul: Two Plays / $3.95
E626	STOPPARD, TOM / Jumpers / $2.95
E726	STOPPARD, TOM / Night and Day / $3.95
E489	STOPPARD, TOM / The Real Inspector Hound and After Magritte: Two Plays / $3.95
B319	STOPPARD, TOM / Rosencrantz and Guildenstern Are Dead / $1.95
E661	STOPPARD, TOM / Travesties / $1.95
E434	VIAN, BORIS / The Generals' Tea Party / $1.95
E62	WALEY, ARTHUR, tr. and ed. / The No Plays of Japan / $5.95

CRITICAL STUDIES

E127	ARTAUD, ANTONIN / The Theater and Its Double / $3.95
E441	COHN, RUBY, ed. / Casebook on Waiting for Godot / $4.95
E603	HARRISON, PAUL CARTER / The Drama of Nommo: Black Theater in the African Continuum / $2.45
E695	HAYMAN, RONALD / How To Read A Play / $2.95
E387	IONESCO, EUGENE / Notes and Counternotes: Writings on the Theater / $3.95

Grove Press, Inc., 196 West Houston Street, New York, N.Y. 10014

DATE DUE